sean burn

we write as burn, *make art, perform, sound as gobscure, use plural as reflection on our broken-mind. we are artistic associate with live theatre newcastle for 2023c.e.*

Burn was previously an artistic associate with Disability Arts Online and Museum of Homelessness (MoH) – both lived experiences; disruptor-in-residence at Edinburgh Printmakers, supported by Future's Venture Foundation (a radical independent art fund); literary fellow at Scotland's writing centre; and NewBridge Project residency. Solo exhibitions internationally, including Alma Zevi Venice; two *Sound&Music* awards; sound-walk commission from the Auxiliary Teesside; online music theatre for GIFT festival and Sage Gateshead. Novella; poetry collections; *Society of Authors* award for *you've already survived - mental distress & healing along the afon wysg* (river usk). *Capital plays* award; Royal Court writers' attachment; *cutter* was 'play of the year for young people' *Time Out*); *collector of tears* was 'play of the year' and *joey* was 'experiment of the year' (both *British Theatre Guide*) and a New Wolsey Theatre *Testing Ground* commission toured in association with Greyscale theatre.

First published in the UK in 2023 by Aurora Metro Publications Ltd.

80 Hill Rise, TW10 6UB, UK

www.aurorametro.com   info@aurorametro.com

mad(e) © 2023 Sean Burn

cutter © 2023 Sean Burn

Cover image © 2023 gobscure

Cover design © 2023 Aurora Metro Publications Ltd.

Production: Yasmeen Doogue-Khan

ISBN: 978-1-912430-93-2 print

ISBN: 978-1-912430-94-9 ebook

mad(e)
&
cutter

by

sean burn

AURORA METRO BOOKS

With thanks to:

Maria Thomas; my therapist; Museum of Homelessness; the folks (too many no longer with us) behind the truth we are 'made not mad'; Joy Hibbins and Suicide Crisis Centre; and of course Yasmin Sidwha and Mandala Theatre

CONTENTS

sean burn. Photo: picturesbybish

made(e) by sean burn tours as follows in 2023:

25-27 January	The North Wall, Oxford
1-2 February	MAST Mayflower Studios, Southampton
9-10 February	The Hat Factory, Luton
21-24 February	London Metropolitan University
2-3 March	Belgrade Theatre, Coventry
7 March	Oxford Brookes University
14-18 March	Pleasance, London
21-25 March	Theatre Deli, Sheffield
30 March	Arts Centre Washington, Sunderland

The play will additionally tour to schools. To book a performance contact: yasmin@mandalatheatre.co.uk

Cast and Crew

Sean Burn	Writer
Yasmin Sidwha	Director
Clarisse Zamba	beira
Lex Stephenson	ash
Max McMillan Ngwenya	kei
Nelvin Kiratu	x.o.dus
Marie-Louise Flexen	Movement Director
Gobscure	Sound Designer
Tazi Amey	Technical Stage Manager
Ryan Clune	Producer
Sophie Lovell-Smith	Set Designer
Paul Batten	Set Maker

With thanks to:

Maria Thomas and Jason Adam who played beira and ash in R&D; film-maker Ben Johnston; workshop tutor / spoken word artist Kema Daley; photographer Stu Allsopp; Josh and Vicky at Graeae; Jess and Matt at MoH; and Euton Daley.

This script is being published before the play tours so might vary slightly from the performed version.

This play was funded by Arts Council England Grants for the Arts

Supported using public funding by

**ARTS COUNCIL
ENGLAND**

Mandala Theatre Company

Mandala Theatre Company is an Oxford-based, national and international touring and training company that creates visceral theatre, giving a voice to those whose stories are not heard and making them visible. It offers pathways to young people from Black, Asian, ethnically diverse, and White working-class backgrounds into the arts. Mandala becomes an Arts Council England National Portfolio Organisation in 2023.

mad(e) is generously supported by Arts Council England, National Lottery Community Fund, Oxford Brookes University – Think Human Festival, Oxford City Council, Oxford Cultural Education Partnership (OXCEP), Oxfordshire Youth, Graeae Theatre Company, Joy Hibbins – Suicide Crisis Centre, MAST Mayflower Studios, The North Wall Arts Centre, The Culture Trust Luton, Belgrade Theatre, Sunderland Culture, Chilworth House School, and Makespace Oxford.

Yasmin Sidhwa

Founder and Artistic Director of Mandala, Yasmin has toured internationally with the Royal National Theatre Company, Tara Arts and Aquila Theatre Companies. She directed and produced numerous theatre productions as Creative Learning Director at Pegasus Theatre, Oxford, for seventeen years. Yasmin was founder and director of MESH – a bi-annual International Youth

Arts festival hosted by Pegasus working with international organisations from Europe and beyond. She has directed all of Mandala's professional shows to date. She co-ran Artivism – international digital and live festival funded by the British Council, with Ashtar Theatre, Ramallah, Palestine, in July 2021. (*blood oil* by the author of *mad(e)*) was part of Artivism and is still available online).

mad(e)

sean burn

This play was commissioned by and first performed by Mandala Theatre Company at the North Wall Oxford, January 2023. Directed by Yasmin Sidwha.

Characters: all working class / underclass / benefits class.

kei – global majority lad, bi, homeless. (their objects – a bivvy-bag for stargazing). humour is their release.

x.o.dus – global majority lad, no recourse to public fund. cook. (objects – bag of homeland soil. also gifted angela davis tee-shirt and santoku knife)

beira – female and not-white, ancient though might appear in their thirties or so.

ash – white lad. carries urn containing their best mate's ash everywhere. inventor.

glitch happens at various moments – e.g. when 'magical' words / ideas are spoken. glitch is otherworld-eerie-flicker. puckish / impish / ariel. glitch is so beyond any other characters' experience that it can scare. glitch can be light, sound, props, shadow, other effects. tableaux from 'beyond' revealing wing / claw / beak; storm of feathers / bird-chorus (please give cast bird-calls); lights-dancing (dlite magic lights!); flame (magic tricks); strong scent (lots of released incense); surface sound change (suddenly walking on pebbles / snow / glass) though surface is unchanged (pre-record or use (e.g.) baking trays with pebbles) and another character 'walkin alongside'.) language glitches – from mishearing words to pitch-change to beautiful glitch when 'male' and 'female' voices speak in unison. a length of honeysuckle offering its flowers / nectar is nurturing glitch. psychologically? 'psychosis' (we've lived experience) – voice – hearing / visions / skin sensations / smells etc. can be brought by extremes of trauma (ptsd); triggered by tiredness, stress, grieving etc. different cultures offer different interpretations. glitch reveals what lies outside the familiar.

Time & Settings:

from valentine's day to calan gaef (1st nov) plus glitch.
city, far from london. overgrown victorian graveyard (acts as nature reserve), off west road.
ghost bus stop (abandoned #1 bus stop on west road).
'the spoon' (early till late cafe), near west road.
murmurations of starlings (spring / autumn), screaming swifts (summer), crows year-round.
even in no wind trees move / scrape against bridges, buses, shops, schools, windows.

one. valentine's day is over

valentine's day is over (june tabor / oysterband version) plays.

performers' backs to us / hands around themselves – flirty, as if each were a couple.

kei eventually breaks this image.

kei   the valentine express south.
               oh kei, what were yu thinkin chuggin energy drink after energy drink on that train?
               cherry-rockstar-brawl, guarana-mutha, live-for-the-madness-cola-organic.
               now yer dyin for a piss only *(chanting)* carls-beerg-carls-beergs block train aisles ...

oldfeller's punchin inside me head *(imitating)* 'man up!'

shove those pussys out the way, only kei never could show whose boss.

instead desperately holdin-piss-in until kings cross piss-trough...

only ma dates photos unreal, run thru station barriers, no time to piss-trough, security eyeballin me as gang-member?

life's no fairy-tale

glitch

kei story-tells, beira is security, the scene is acted out together

kei   trip, ko'd to concrete, piss maself n ma prince charmin ghosts.

security helps me up

beira *(as security)* hot-choc n lemon-muffin, look like yu could do with sugar-hit

kei   way more love than the oldfeller.

oh kei, why tell yer oldfeller

valentine's a london lad?

joe lycett me, bi totally.

oldfeller hits us

with *(imitating)* valentine's day n not chasin pussy then yer takin the piss n i'm thrown to the road.

blub this to security who fixes me with

beira *(as security)* return n thaw that oldfeller's heart –

kei   been wantin love since i wz wee.

the oldfeller will say kei yer pretty.

one beery-night he flaps wrists n lisps kei-ty, katy n girlie-kei becomes goalpost for pot-shots with his mates, celebration-drink each time they hit little-kei in the balls – learnin age nine, cemetery past ma house is only place i'm fittin ... northbound train carlsbee-eeergs, the late bus vom-rocketin past oldfeller's house, but kei is keyless n so make ma way to cemetery *(showing)* carryin this bivvy, bivouac bag, waterproof n better than any sleepin bag.

achin for star-gazin n romance in this bivvy-bag for ever – now i bed down alone tucked away in tangle ov ash tree, ivy n bramble in corner ov a knackered graveyard with only fox, owl, hedgehog, fallen leaves n empty energy-drink cans for company

kei tucks in accompanied by glitch, a 'magic noise-event' – owl, distant fox, drink cans, leaves and paper whisper

elsewhere ash trickles ash from hand into his urn and back

x.o.dus chalks their angela davis tee-shirt slogan large enough so all read clearly: 'we have to talk about liberating minds as well as liberating society'

kei   alone in this tangle ov tree, ivy n fern –
                 life's endin before yu even began oh kei...
                 oh shit, desperate for a piss, why folx call it a slash,
                 slash is well violent...
                 wish i could remain undercover but...

glitch – all urgently need to piss, kei struggling to get out of bivvy-bag

pisstroughers (lads chorus of peacock-struts, fly-unzippings, eyes dead ahead)

pisstrougers carlsbeeeerg carlsbeeerg slaaash – be a bloody
                  ma-an,

stare dead ahead, don't get yer head kicked i-in, head kicked i-in

eyeballin another pisstrougher makes yu gay

beira *(joining the pisstroughers)* oi oi girlie-man, best yu can? this is how wolves whistle

beira's wolf whistle deafens the lads, she controls them now

beira   sistah-mam-nan on her knees scrub-scrubbin yer pisstrough while

dead-ahead the ad reads: that really yer babby?

yer lass could be cheatin.

get dna tested.

£79, no hidden fees.

stop seein us as witch-bitch – *(glitch)*...

see instead yer sistah-man-nan scared by yer swagger-dagger n knackered thru tryin to keepin yu's outta trouble

unglitch

x.o.dus and ash now separately head for 'the spoon'

kei *(stashing a means to end his life – we don't see clearly what)* hollowed out, empty, oh kei, no-one's here for ya, no-one will hear ya

ash and x-o-dus are now in 'the spoon' being served by beira

beira *(to ash)* graveyard with yer mash?

ash   whaaat?

beira *(to ash)* graveyard ... with ... yer ... mash?

ash   w.t.f?

beira   gravy over yer ash?

ash *(angrily shoving the urn he carries at her)* yu takin the piss?

beira   there's others queuein, now make up yer mind, gravy over yer mash?

ash	oh, right, pp-pplease
beira	n scrapins – bone – tombstone?
ash	yu are messin with ma mind witch, why?

glitch

beira/x.o.dus *(speaking together ghostly)* witch? glitch! seer oracle
> enchantress charm-binder voodoo.
> where-wen will yer fury end poor-lad ash?

ash freaks into dropping urn

x.o.dus considerately wipes urn down with his angela davis tee, goes to hand urn back

ash grabs urn and tee-shirt, knocking x.o.dus down (swift, not considered violence)

ash   grassin to council there's rats in yer food grassin to feds illegals work here, got no need to burn yer cafe 'the spoon' down

beira throws fire at ash (flash paper magic trick) who runs off

x.o.dus   takes shirt off ma back – shirt which reads 'we have to talk about liberating minds as well as liberating society'

beira *(handing ash's food to x.o.dus)* eat

x.o.dus *(taps head)* family recipes. let us cook here!

beira   x.o.dus. eat first!

x.o.dus   *(eating through this conversation)* haven't told ma name

beira   yu are x.o.dus

x.o.dus   yu aren't feds – state – border??

beira   beira kens no border in shapin mountain n whirlpool, in collectin firewood thru freeze n thaw.

beira is giantess n gentleness both.

n yu have been a long-time comin x.o.dus

x.o.dus feds, they stamp NRPF, no recourse to public funds, i have no money. let me cook

beira poor-lad ash is too scared to grass – he kens we'd call cailleach down

x.o.dus ca-yee-lleach? please

beira cailleach is storm raised to drive away the grey. beira will help yu recover shirt taken off yer back.

right now tho? time to gather firewood!

beira brings a storm of possibilities

lads dance to english black boys (by x.o.dus) while beira gathers firewood

two. shakespeare's-birthday-slash-st george's day (23rd april)

ash	england – angerland st george flag flies today
x.o.dus	frost flags with blood-slash grow overnight
kei	st george's day is shakspeare's birthday.
	shakepere, yu've heard ov her!
beira	23 april. st george's day for some on this soil
kei	shakespeare spelt her name 6 different ways.
	wz pottymouth bi. n racist fact.
	but she found the flow
ash	england angerland st george flag flies today
x.o.dus	reach out to touch that blooded flag n a leerbelly shouts
all	whatchoostarinat?
kei	shakespeare's laffin her tits off at how posh-boys mangle her flow
beira	saint george was a soldier in palestine – israel
kei	no-ones charged saint george for slayin an endangered species?
beira	23rd april n a european first sees the shoreline ov brazil.
	coca cola change the formulae, quickly change it back.
	hitler receives a telegram, an incel attacks, inventors ov diets die.
	a king is crowned, later they die strainin on the bogs.
	cardiff beat arsenal in a cup final.
kei	how hard it is to not want revenge -
	all laugh wen yu tickle us – bleed wen yu prick us – all blood is red

lads form pisstroughers and march and chant

pisstroughers   wat-chachacha-stari-nat

pisstroughers hurl each actor forward in turn and noise-event them – cops' IC codes are allocated to each – director yasmin is IC4

pisstroughers   take back control takin back control we are takin control

> not from round here n yer food stinks
> takin our white girls?
> actin in our pornos?
> why so angry?
> interrogate interrogate
> wrong clothes wrong hair wrong time n place
> outside yer ghetto so yer wrong place defo
> too loud too urban n yer attitudes criminal
> IC2. IC3. IC4. IC5. IC6. IC x IC x IC x

IC code of x.o.dus is chanted while they are ejected from group

> cha-foookilooki-nat, backlash backlash, feel the lash
> boats that way and get that hair under control

x.o.dus is swallowed back into group

> interrogate interrogate IC x IC x IC x

IC code of beira is chanted while they are ejected from group

> too much cheek n warpaints way too loud
> IC6. IC5. IC4. IC3. IC2. sluts askin for it yer honour

beira is swallowed back into group

> interrogate – IC x IC x IC x

IC code of kei is chanted while they are ejected from group

glitterball, pillowbiter, yer cruisin-to-bruisins,
graveyard over ghetto everyway,
sketchy mofo yu should be crim
- bring back clause 28

kei is swallowed back into group

ash/ *(ash throws himself out shouting)* IC1 IC1 IC1 IC1 IC1 IC1
    IC1
pisstroughers/ de-escalate boy – get back in the line-up – get
    back in line

*beira sings verses 4 – 8 of 'in the ghetto' (elvis presley) and
others join in*

*(alternatively Candi Staton's version of those verses plays as
the cast perform physically)*

then...

kei   diss us n roast us – why's there always gotta be
               beef?
               that way all go facedown – all need relief
               we all bleed wen yu prick us, laugh wen yu tickle us
               so instead render tender deeds ov mercy yeah?
beira *(kissing kei's head)* gentleness as yer strategy?
               beiras proud to ken yu

three. spring madness

x.o.dus at 'the spoon', kei bivvying in graveyard, ash with urn at '#1' bus stop –

it's a hostile environment

beira	spring sap rises, hares box, robins punch out each others lights n lads ache to fight jes like their oldfeller.
	one unexpected punch fells n from this chaos grows
kei	feel. be held. become un-numbed
beira	flow ov folx is always to these lushlands – why hostile environments feel the need to punch?
	witness how chaos grows
x.o.dus	nrpf no public funds i pay ma way numbed by others hate
beira	winter keeps greenshoots safe underground, if the sun punches
	too soon, all feel the burn
ash	shoutin be a man, stop cryin, whatchoo-starin at, how this body numbs
beira	this springs heat punchin too hard too fast
lads *(each surfaces from their nightmare in their own zone)*	un-numb / take this numbness away / to feeeel!
x.o.dus	i am eight now so nearly a man.
	for so long da doesn't hug hold
	say he loves me, no fun. gran says
beira *(as gran)*	let's trick da into kiss me hold me hug me say he loves me.
x.o.dus	gran learns me in how to trick da.
	so excited it makes me do ma best foot-to-foot dance ... now no more foot-dance, i'd sooner end it than be taken by border control, gone i wish

glitch (on wish) – sudden roaring chainsaws etc. and a tree branch is thrown onstage)

ash *(shouting)* no cash to carlsberg-drown-sorrow at the dyin
ov ma best, only mate karl – nothin's left but ash-
grey-numb, wish i was gone

glitch (as before, branch is thrown onstage)

kei *(mocking)* yer call is precious ... not!

yu can't even *(air-quotes)* 'signpost' me for housin
till yer app gets fundin ... at least have the guts n
terminate me, wiiish!

glitch as before, branch is thrown onstage

beira *(gathering these branches as firewood)* firewood to warm
the cold times.

yu gag for warmin sun but long winters keep
greenshoots safe.

balance is needed to counter man's drive for
growth n yeah it is man, suited-booted, greenback-
greenback-greenback

(as quizshow host) who's the daddy?

welcome to the quiz-show with balls!

3 random bad-boys man-up enough at the
pisstrough n walk off with enough greenback – roll
– loot for the strides – whip – witch ov their dreams
... *(crooking / waggling little finger)* but pussy out?

i rip hairs out yer butt-crack ... sooo which big-
spenders are steppin to the pisstrough tonight?

who's the daddy?

beira hunts pisstroughers ash, kei, x.o.dus who are hiding in the audience

beira   yu, yu n yu!

all   *(chanting)* greenback-greenback-greenback

beira	three king-kong ding-dong no-holds-barred rounds: *(holding mid-finger up first)* starters; *(two fingers flicking v's)* meat n veg; *(now three fingers)* puddin; y'all get one amuse-bouche to rip yer enemys gonads, so channel yer piers organ!
beira	ash, yer starter: spill x.o.dus' biggest fear
ash	security rough-n-tumblin him to ground cos they see a big-brute
beira	meat n veg!
	gay, soz kei's fear volunteerin at west road food bank?
ash	homeless, washin with wet-wipes, someone's gonna say he stinks
beira	n puddin!
	yu like puddin daddybod-ash ... ooh kei's playin amuse-bouche, he's ready to dish
kei	moobs, man-boobs, ash in the mirror terrified he's gettin curvier
x.o.dus	*(playing amuse bouche)* ash tellin only mate, lass yer tryin to pull?
	jump from the singin bridge to show yer man enough ... karl leaps n ash ends youtubin his mates last breath in river below
beira	who's the daddy?
	ain't yu ash, yer loser same as x.o.dus n kei... *(ditching game-show)* glamour ain't gold, go tell yer mate, bro or oldfeller no lech or sleaze, no means no always – fairy-tale traditionally offer 3 wishes
ash	wish i told mate karl how much i looked up to 'em
kei	wishin for love, lad-lass-in between-beyond-don't matter love is love
x.o.dus	wish this country would have ma back
beira	have yer own backs.

wen mates-fathers-the state dick around, tell 'em stop numb-spread-carlsberg-splainin.

go wisely in all ways n always

unglitch. glamour of quizshow fades

x.o.dus   excited by gran practicin me in trickin da i do ma best foot-to-foot hop-dance

beira *(as gran)* yu n me are the same, the same slim.
now walk-grin-cackle like gran

x.o.dus   practice walkin grinnin cacklin like gran.
in her clothes so softly nice
lovin her smell on me

beira *(as gran)* i do yer hair like mine

x.o.dus   she tricks ma hair just like hers

beira *(as gran)* in the flickery dark da won't see the difference

x.o.dus   age eight in flickery-dark i am gran – wishin for this trick to work

glitch on word 'wish' brings them to now, in 'the spoon'

beira   the spoon cafe will shelter yu x.o.dus

beira offers santoku knife to x.o.dus who reacts badly

beira   yu asked to cook here? this is tool only

x.o.dus   choose wisely, yu did say

beira   japanese. santoku.
multi-purpose. chop, dice, slice, spread, pare.
brittle metal so blade likely snaps if used in haste

x.o.dus   i choose wise, to cook, i won't let yu down

x.o.dus takes the santoku knife, bows to beira

beira *(kisses side of x.o.dus' head)* yer ancestors are proud

beira shows x.o.dus what he needs to know about the spoon

ash is at the '#1' bus stop / kei walks past

ash   oi i said oi oi oi

kei   do i know yu?

ash   yu were in ma head pisstroughin

kei   yu were havin *that* dream?

ash   pisstroughin next to me n yu start turnin yer head?!

kei   yu were havin *that* dream!

ash   get outta ma head freak

kei   wz yu doin the dreamin hun

ash lunges at kei who gets away

x.o.dus   in the flickery-dark i am gran ... da kisses gran on the cheek only it is me even tho he won't ever kiss his boy age eight a man now.

        keep hop-dance inside. da hugs gran. it is still me. now gran walks out. two grans.

        da's been to get eggs for special ... he crunches egg in hand – the biggest cruuuunch – smears egg across ma face.

        grow-up grow-up grow-up. ... i grow up ... numb

beira   *(disappears through a glitch)* one crunch causin such chaos, a wee road-

        trip to bring balance back, try beira, gotta try!

four. summer heat

x.o.dus preps / cooks flatbread in 'the spoon', the gifted santoku knife prominent

ash is with urn elsewhere, kei in a third space stargazing

x.o.dus *(direct address)* flatbread is the ultimate migrant, slippin every border, cheap n on every tongue. flatbread is latinx – jewish – north african n east ... iberian – mediterranean – middle east – islamic – south asian.

add yer regions spice – fenugreek – garlic – berbere – zaatar.

egg / no egg?

savoury or sweet?

butter-n-honey or yoghurt-cucumber-olive oil. flatbread mops meat n veg so no washin up. eat flatbread n yu have to down weapons cos yer hands will be full.

x.o.dus produces a fist of soil wrapped in paper, translucent with oil which he unwraps

x.o.dus family recipe is all i have left ... apart from this crumble-fist ov homeland soil

kei eat or freeze? global heatin means i don't freeze. clouds n linins.

jo-oo-oke tho sickly true.

the oldfeller tells mate little-kei has girl's hips – oldfeller's cuttin little-kei's hair short n rough till ears bleed –

sports day rippin off ribbons little-kei won cos they're girlie ...

these voices mean kei's up n over bridge-edge n folx are shoutin jump

- n then i freeze –

fly off this bridge n the oldfeller will disown ma coffin – the last laugh his

kei   as i'm frozen this fire-fighter with rainbow-braces hauls me back sayin

beira *(as firefighter)*   yu are better than this

kei   we are better than this

beira *(as firefighter)*   we are all better than this

beira makes a shooting star (d-lites) which little-kei catches

little-kei plays with magic (d-lites) lights, comforted by graveyard sounds

x.o.dus slowly unwraps soil and inhales, finally 'there'

x.o.dus   da says cookin is weakness

beira *(as gran)* let's trick da – only better this time.

      put on ma cookin-top so no mess gets on yer – da will never guess yer the cook

x.o.dus   how i love smellin ov yer gran.

      to pour water into semolina – stir n warm slow-slow, ten minutes till all froths.

      now i dance foot-to-foot a whole hour how long it takes to cool before the next part ov the trick

ash unwraps urn, puts on angela davis tee-shirt, talks to urn

ash   skivin school for the sand-dunes n sea, so much warmth n colour yu brought karl-mate.

      yu sayin 'let's chill' n we do.

      pushin past the reeds that hid those old war tank-traps.

findin the wide horizoned sea beyond where our
river spills. plantin driftwood upright.

n watchin the blood sky above...

was like yu were my brother karl, n yu were –
runnin into the sea n runnin out again shock ov the
cold n now i freeze bollocks off while yer under for
all time, swap with yer anytime

ash heads for 'the spoon' as

x.o.dus *(direct address)* an hour ov hop-dance ... at last i can
add more n more flour, a little sugar, a tiny salt, a
pinch yeast, n fluff-fluff-fluff all with more water – n
then a half-hour hop-dancin – at last

beira *(as gran)* now yu can peek ... tell me

x.o.dus   yeeesss, the bubbly-fluff has grown

beira *(as gran – kissing into x.o.dus' head)* good job, no
lumps

kei   that rainbow-brace-firefighter is in foodbank queue
... they refuse to catch ma eye wen i help out ... long
to say i ken a cafe, the spoon, eat with me, ma treat,
it's warm, i am lonely, yu are cute ...

x.o.dus   bubble with pride as i wipe oil into the hot hot pan
with this paper

*(shows soil-holdin-paper translucent from cookin
oil)*

circle bubbly-fluff on n bubbles appear – stack these
with butter n honey n life is sweet – serve gran then
da who smiles yu cook good for a man

kei *(heading for cafe)* these days too many are screamin jump.
would yu share yer last food with a starvin tory?
i'd cram food into their gob just to stop the lies

x.o.dus   that last night i am last ov ma fam n fatten myself
on all the eggs-honey-butter – one last flatbread to
one side for ancestors, gran n dad too now – n then

i burn n burn everythin, soldier will never lie under grans roof – scoop this fist ov soil – never look back – recipe here *(taps head)*, n with this gift ov san-to-ku knife – i spread – slice – chop – dice – fillet – make beira proud

ash (tee-shirt visible) arrives at 'the spoon' and slams urn on counter

x.o.dus, startled, grabs knife in defence

ash leaps back as kei arrives and they collide

ash *(seeing kei)* stay outta ma dreams yu nightmarin freak
kei *(blowing kiss)* girl, yu are so undreamt

ash kicks off, x.o.dus then steps into ash

santoku knife is dropped as they struggle over tee-shirt

ash	cook british
kei	balti? pizza? chinese? sushi? fish n chips is jewish!
x.o.dus	that tee-shirt off ma back? i'm takin it back
kei	'the spoon' is shut
ash	who made yu god?

kei unscrews urn, throws ash in both their faces, rams knife into urn ash

kei	close up!

x.o.dus does

ash	mental, crazy, mofo could-ov killed me
kei	shhh or i unleash more vesuvius – krakatoa – montserrat

ash flinches as kei goes to throw more ash

x.o.dus	i cook is all ... yer both famished.

here. ma best buttery-hot. eat

x.o.dus butters, tears and shares flatbread with kei, both eat

ash is reluctant but does finally eat

x.o.dus   i am touchin england

beira *(as firefighter, handin x.o.dus clothes)* yu've travelled far, welcome, dry clothes

x.o.dus   en-gland?

beira *(as firefighter)* yer new home ... put dry clothes on

x.o.dus   yu wear rainbows here!

beira *(as firefighter)* welcome to the land ov rainbows

x.o.dus *(pointing at ash)* that takes shirt off ma back

ash   yu near knifed me

x.o.dus   knife is to slice-dice-chop-fillet-spread only – can break if stabbed

kei   yu both fought

x.o.dus *(crying)* so shamed i scare, forget knife, wantin what is mine

beira *(offstage)* one unexpected punch fells n from this chaos grows

x.o.dus   yu eat ma bread

ash   given freely

kei   so this is slavery-time still?

beira *(offstage)* droppin yer fist has way more power

kei hugs x.o.dus

when x.o.dus stops crying, kei releases him

kei *(joking at ash)* yu next for cuddles mofo

ash   dickhead

kei   in yer dreams

ash   don't want yer dirty arms

kei   yu see black-lad n yer go-to is aggro

ash   never shoutin jump ... again

beira   alright lads! jump to it!

pisstroughers *(military drill which falls apart)*

      rugger-bugger – shock-jock – pumped-up!

      forget good cop bad cop, be bad-cop then worse!

      be burke&hare, buff tony blair, boris n johnson (ancient news)

      boys will be boys ... but if they won't carlsber-rrrg?

      ken there's more 'n 2 sides to each – coin – tale – river – border-wall -

      rugger bugger off, give virile the snip, men-o-war nah!

      pretty-boy, femme, nerd, beggarman, grief – don't hide yer tears –

      break all binaries – rambo or rimbaud?

      poet rimbaud had the flow, frank ocean has the flow, joe lycett knows – n killer mike n el-p?

      rtj is hardcore muthahugger truelove

unglitch

kei *(at ash)* without lookin down describe the tee-shirt yer wearin

when ash goes to look down, kei tips ash's head back up

ash hates being touched

ash   uuh black chick?

kei   yer dissin one ov this century's finest minds!

kei traces the tee-shirt slogan across ash's moobs, freaking ash right out

kei   inked across yer moobs is 'we have to talk about liberating minds as

	well as liberating society'
ash	b.g.t? song? she is off the box?
kei	rollin stones sang about professor angela davis. proud n out lesbian.

times named her world's top hundred.

yu n yrs name her most
wanted, almost *(throat-slitting gesture)*...

jack this shirt off x.o.dus' back but can't be arsed readin what's inked?! ... *(stripping top off a terrified ash)* say her name whiteboy! say. her. name.

x.o.dus / beira *(layered voices producing eerily beautiful glitch)*

we have to talk about liberating minds as well as liberating society

we have to talk about liberating minds as well as liberating society

we have to talk about liberating minds as well as liberating society

beira   one unexpected punch fells n from this chaos grows – withhold the expected blow is way more powerful.

return from wee roadtrip n find yu fine lads turnin bakers n peace-makers – each cailleach – witch – seer – oracle – charmbinder – voodoo – fury – is proud ov such inkings

all   'we have to talk about liberating minds as well as liberating society' –

beira kisses kei's head, then summons moonlight benjamin – memwa'n and all dance

five. storm before the calm (fever-dream in autumn heat)

all three lads fail to sleep due to the heat

all   wish someone proud ov me wish i were proud ov
            me wish

glitch (on word wish) brings noise event which beira battles

*lads struggle wordlessly to beira, sheltering their younger
selves and bringin their item*

*noise-event enters (pre-recorded noise / text, including
helicopter, glass-smash, shouts, wagner's 'ride of the valkyries'
– the operatic-war)*

noise-event *(playing wagner's 'valkyries')* dum-da-da-
            der-da dum-da-da-der-da dum-da-da-der-da ...
            carrrlsberrrg!

beira   now get to the front n smash it feller?
            unlearn-unlearn-unlearn

noise-event pinocchio princess pansy get back in that kitchen
            we're starvin ... laws against yu lot should be – push
            back boats bring back clause 28

beira   love poem over threat, love bridges over battle,
            love always yer way –

            a slow army graveyard-grows – rowan n ash n birch
            n alder –

            willow fern bluebell n raspberry – hawthorn oak
            gorse holly bramble

noise-event   / yo bro-alpha rip to the front n smash it, i'm
            mofo yu homo ...

            come over here n say that ... virgin ... beta ... blue-
            pill'er   .   .   .

	dum-da-da-der-da dum-da-da-der-da dum-da-da-der-da
beira	from din ov fist n twist ov shank unfurl yer fists n ask for help
noise-event	cry-baby whiner ... i am fantastic, yu fat n dyspraxic
beira	ligatures round yer necks?
	untie!
noise-event	whupp yer ass red pills gonna this stud owns ya
beira	holly leaves rip yer manosphere – tree-roots trip yer – fruits seduce yer – ferns unfurl yer love
noise-event	snot-nose-whiner will four-chan yer, muck-mag-studs gonna dominate yer / dum-da-da-der-da dum-da-da-der-da
beira	/ yellerin must stop, roots crack concrete!
	bark hug yer, leaf n relief
	break yer fall
noise-event	/ dum-da-da-der-da dum-da-da-der-da terminate yer
beira	/ tree-bark hug yer close, root-crack yer toxic masculinity, leaf n relief
	break yer fall raspberry fruit seduce yer fern unfurl loooove

beira breaks the noise-event and lads arrive with their 'transitional objects'

these items get shown hauntingly gently to the environment

nature (feathers / leaves etc.) are stroked on them, secrets whispered into them. finally the items are rocked, hugged – all cry as they care for their younger self. hammock 'then the quiet explosion' is the track for this

beira	ken yu all are missed, are loved, always will be.

tell yer wee yer younger selves safe now ... tell wee
ash, wee kei, wee x.o.dus all is safe ... this slow army
ov tree is witness so go ahead

kei   little kei – love yu

ash   little ash – rock yu

x.o.dus   little x.o.dus – yer no longer missin

lads   such futures ahead, love yu, safe now, yu's are safe

x.o.dus   sendin love to yu's family even tho yer now stars
above

beira   all things their season n all for a reason –
relax chillax love let go

kei   oldfeller? still lovin yer tho yer dickhead ways don't
deserve

beira   relax chillax love let go – ken yu wounded healers
are loved

ash   karl yer knob, fuckin love yer

*ash desperately fails to rescue, then holds beira as (dead) karl,
kei is lass – hold this, as*

ash   so sorry lass who wanted yu to pull her instead saw
us pullin yer corpse from river, our film deleted for
'violatin youtube policy'

beira   all is flow. freeze aye but the melt also.
love all flesh n also the crumblin to bone.
wounded healers make the best healers lads ...
now ken yu wounded healers are loved

*beira pulls flowers off a glitch of honeysuckle, gives out their
beads of honey to suck*

beira   this city is the honeys-sucklin, beads ov honey giftin
yu strength ... ask more, question everythin, seek
justice n reparation always n in all ways, love&rage
both ... yu've learnt to have yer own back now have
each other's – the brotherin days are ahead

six. feast of the dead (november 1st – calan gaef (welsh first day of winter))

x.o.dus prepares food, kei assists at 'the spoon'

in the graveyard, beira prepares for apple-bobbing

kei	incels' ugly thoughts mean they're gettin none ... so buy 'em a chunk ov texas n then can get on *(mimes fucking)* mm-mmm each other!
x.o.dus	yer jokes are sick kei
kei	preachers ov hate genst us bi's, fly 'em out as fresh-meat for incel-corner
x.o.dus	gagmaster-yu
kei	drownin street makes me gag.
	prime-minister's demandin henry the eight super-powers ... henry's six wives died beheaded, died, died, beheaded, survived
x.o.dus	what is queen ov winter wantin with yer graveyard this november first?
kei	calan gaef – first day ov winter – walls between worlds are thinnest – *(taps head)* she is good craic
x.o.dus	n ash is always late
kei	fairy-lightin the graveyard

ash enters 'the spoon'

kei	fairy light ash! relaxin with a rainbow
ash	yu cruisin for a bruisin?
kei	so not in ma dreams still
x.o.dus	both yu's chill
ash	didn't deserve to live after karl ... wimped out, couldn't even end it, jes hurtin maself to numb
x.o.dus	we all need some numb
kei	so true

x.o.dus *(pointing to urn)* yer ash is safe. n yu are too

ash   still hurts

kei   'there is no hierarchy ov suffering.' audre lorde

ash   another tee-shirt?

kei   it's not b.g.t.

x.o.dus   chill!

kei   there is still no hierarchy ov sufferin tho yeah?

ash   had this moment up the graveyard

x.o.dus / *(simultaneous with kei)* shite / bloodied?

kei / *(simultaneous with x.o.dus)* yu needin plasters?

ash   all's good man – those moments wen head-fog clears?...

let's never use the word suicide again yeah, nuke it, gone – tell the truth about what actually did us in – death cos our hearts are bleedin? mine for karl, yrs x.o.dus for dead fam, kei yer da don't deserve yer love ... life ends cos we have no roof, no money, no future ... i'm s'posed to hate yu kei yu bloody fairy?

kei   half-fairy

ash   n hate yu x.o.dus for comin over here n cookin such lush bloody food?

the word suicide's gone!

tell the truth – death by poverty or disability ... death by piers organ – prince andrew – twitter – trump ..

prime minister too lazy to push us under the bus still causes our deaths

kei   get sectioned, that's yer get outta jail.

they'll have to unlock yu pronto

ash   callin me sane? that bloody hurts!

kei   bloody respect ash

thirteen drumbeats, a summons from beira

beira *(off)* ashes ashes, dust n dust, winter's callin, come yer
                 must
kei   can't keep queen ov winter waitin lads

they set off with flatbreads

suddenly a mari lwyd nightmares them towards graveyard

*mari lwyd is a ghostly white horse (noisy jawbone, sheet,
decoration, harness bells etc.) and part of the welsh tradition
of calan gaef)*

in the graveyard beira throws off the mari lwyd

beira	look on yer faces lads!
	hope yer boxers are still clean
lads	un-funny
beira	wen yer as old as me yu gotta get yer laughs
x.o.dus	how old are yu?
kei	thirty?
ash	forty!
beira	five thousand / give or take
lads	/ cracked – crazy – doolally
beira	welcome to calan gaef – first ov winter – walls ov the worlds are thinner than yu can imagine ... so imagine yer deaths
lads	yer mad?!
beira	made not mad ... we all are ... made not mad

*beira writes mad in chalk in the graveyard, pauses, then adds a
letter 'e' to read made)*

beira   first day ov winter this crone – witch – hag –
                   ancestor – seer – asks yu to trust her with yer
                   deaths imaginins...

summer to winter, wax to wane, again-n-again, greenshoot sleeps deep under protected until time to grow, at last to feast, love&ragin both ... so tell!

kei keep imaginin dyin among this graveyards fox n owl n hedgehog n fallen leaves n empty energy drink cans n not bein found for weeks

till ma corpse-stink finally freaks some unlucky finder out – sick for wishin me oldfeller found me rotted corpse?

kei clutches heart and pretends coronary / dying – all 'piss' themselves laughing

beira bleak humour gets yu thru bleakest times. at yer lowest then bring on yer sickest jokes.

desperate to avoid dyin we forget to live.

how dya wanna be remembered ash?

ash don't wanna ghost, slip thru cracks, wanna be remembered

beira how?

ash imagine a sea burial reef built from cement-dust n karl-ash n crushed-rubbish rockin the map from cardiff to swansea, carlisle to stranraer, sunderland n hartlepool n hull.

this reef ov ashes is for seaweed to root to, shells to fix to, crabs to scuttle under – a reef that brings fish, memory, n seagrass that locks up carbon's pollution

beira magnificent, many many futures, givin such hope

x.o.dus n folx will need food to build ash's reef – n i want to crack up at kei's jokes

beira on this first day ov winter yu lads finally wanna live? n live better!

soon i receive those gifts yu all have brought

lads yu said nothin about gifts

beira   times comin to give up what has burdened yu's all for too long

lads *(realising)* naaaaah!

beira   ken yu are loved lads ken yu are all loved *(overwhelming)* now

glitch (remember beira is force of nature – unstoppable)

beira drags all three to the water – dunks them, makes them apple-bob until each lad helps one another to surface with apple in gob (cheating encouraged)

beira   first day ov winter is never all fun n light n i'm so worn by this year

            (she hands envelope over)

            the spoons in yer hands, this paper makes yu custodians, a brotherhood to plot plan laugh food fun sanctuary.

            now give up yer gifts before i sleep, prove 3 wise men are more than myth!

kei produces bivvy and tucks beira in

kei   i can kip at the spoon so i won't be needin this

ash unscrews urn, unsure

kei fake-sneezes, tricking ash into scattering ash

x.o.dus unwraps soil, throws this into the mix

there is a storm of soil, ash, leaves, more

this cloud of glitch should mesmerise (smell of honeysuckle too)

lads   yu will be back

            yu'd better bloody be comin back

            yu are loved beira know yu are all loved

the chaos-cloud of glitch clears

beira has left behind a mound with some green growth

peatbog faeries 'spiders' plays and the lads dance together and off

lights down

the end.

cutter

sean burn

cutter was commissioned and toured by Half Moon Theatre, in autumn 2004 and named *Time Out*'s 'Play of the Year for Children and Young People' that year. Directed by Vishni Velada Billson.

Characters:

granda – *trinidadian. in his 60's.* played by Richie Campbell

cutter – *dual heritage granddaughter. 18.* played by Maria Thomas

one. swansea bay

granda   swansea bay, ma wee bright star, swansea bay. what do we see?

cutter *(cartwheeling, a child)* a butterfly dancin on autumn sand granda

granda   two halves a cockleshell kissin

cutter   look a cowrie.

a cowrie granda, a cowrie

granda   in the caribbean when i was a lad – cowries the size of yr hand.

here, cold water make 'em small so small ma wee star

cutter   and another cowrie, granda.

and another and another!

granda   wee miracles like yu ... what else?

cutter   the feel of sand between ma toes it's like ... a song!

granda   smell the sea!

taste its beauty, ma mornin star

cutter   the song of stars and shingle and surf and gulls.

granda   music of this, our kingdom of the invisible.

look: a watch with no batteries.

the tickin of waves.

soon we'll need to find out the time

cutter   and coal granda. coal. see?

what yu dug for

granda   what we dug for aye ... till the wheels stopped. mountains black with the seam.

and men: their faces black as yu as me

cutter   grit and grime and

granda   remember this: they say coal is dirty, but it burns, burns bright, burns with a fierce fierce flame.

crushed for millions of years but still it remembers; see here

cutter leaves! trunk! roots!

granda dreamin from where it came.

remember that child – no matter what others say, no matter what they call yu – coal is beautiful, precious, black.

contains the memory of its beginnin's.

and crushed, it contains power unimagined

cutter diamonds

granda aye ma bright star. diamonds.

a perfect splittin of light; its brilliant blade has a cuttin power beyond imaginin.

never forget child. never forget

cutter never granda. i won't ever forget

two. school

granda *(instructing cutter in boxing)* jab jab left jab right

cutter   so this teacher edward he's askin what the capital
              is, now he's always got it in for me.

granda   jab jab left jab right jab right

cutter   i pipes up cardiff. car-diff? he says and laughs.
              and yu can see the spittle flyin out.
              it's lon-don, child.
              we are all one country now.

granda   hook cut snap yr wrists snap back snap

cutter   or don't yr lot – and here he's liftin ma arm aloft for
              all
              the others to see it dirty like the miners up and out
              their cages only mine won't wash and tho granda
              says stand tough it's hard when yr small and
              teachers wavin yu about like a raggedy-doll.

granda   lon-don

cutter   he spits and i goes but granda says edward slams
              down, slams down his fists on the desk.
              don't defy me. don't trouble-make in ma class.

granda   yu ran from yr class.
              i found yu in our back alley cryin yr wee eyes out
              and when yu tells i roll up sleeves says

granda / cutter   little star, ma little star, there's a time
              to fight

granda   and i marches off to school.
              edward wore dark glasses for weeks

cutter   teacher never did give me grief after tho coppers
              was round causin all kinds...
              a caution the coppers said. and bound over to keep
              the peace, so yu was. bound over!

granda	yu thought they was gonna to tie me up in the yard like next doors dog!
cutter	yu burst out laughin at that. and i sat giddy-uppin giddy-giddy-uppin on yr rough smooth sweet coal-miners back as yu ruffed and romped
granda	took yu down the coast for special treat
cutter	cod and chips and bara brith and walkin the beach and stories and. and a new red ribbon so ma hair didn't flop as i *(cutter cartwheels)*
granda	taught yu principles, tried to ... taught yu belief, i tried
cutter	moved to the big school after. learnin to fight me corner. granda yu taught us
granda	yu got a quick temper, inherited that from yr ma, who got it from me, and i got that from the islands – back then: yu had to stand up for yr family, yr street, yr town: carnival was war!
cutter	how yu'd read that old left-wing newspaper: the mornin star? and i asked what yu readin. so yu took ma hand, guided it to the words, helped me spell 'em out, first thing i ever read was title yr paper
cutter/granda	mo-r-nin star
cutter	yu helped me with ma readin and then it got so i out-read yu, granda ... i helped yu
granda	comin home with all that personal development stuff, askin questions, i couldnt keep up
cutter	we done loads of classes on stuff like ... what's right?
granda	fight yr corner lass.
granda / cutter	*(cutter boxing in time)* jab jab left jab right hook cut jab jab left jab right jab right

        snap yr wrists ... snap back ... snap ... and back
        upper cut and ... and jab right jab right snap and
        snap

cutter   but there's a time to make yr peace too, yeah?

granda   yr growin too fast for me these days, growin too fast

granda/cutter   upper cut and ... and jab right jab right

granda boxing in background as cutter speaks

cutter/granda *(as playground chant)* cu-tter. cu-tter. cut cut cut.
        cu-tter. cu-tter. cut cut cut.

cutter *(as herself)* there's worse names to be called than that.
        want some blood. nuuh? well back off. back. off
        miss jones at high school she was alright, she
        cared, tried to ...

(as teacher) must be hard growin up without yr ma. yr havin a
        tough time?

(as herself)   me granda's fine

(as teacher)   but

(as herself)   but nothin. right?

(as teacher) what about those things only mothers can do?
        he's a good man but maybes?...
        look if there's anythin yu wanna talk about now ...
        later: i'm here for yu

(as herself) but i just couldn't name all those things between a
        mother and her daughter.
        sometimes i don't wanna box, don't wanna fight,
        wanna get ma hair braided up fine and ... tho that
        teacher encouraged us to fight too ... when the time
        was right.
        miss jones came with granda to me first fight.
        told me after how she didn't dare look, kept her
        hands front-of her eyes, she were terrified!
        didn't tell her how i felt ... filled with butterflies!

three. carnival

cutter / granda dressed for carnival. dancing to carnival music

granda reaches into his pocket, pulls out a locket. places it round cutter's neck

granda   was yr ma's.
cutter   i remember, i remember.
granda   yr ma, ma daughter. it's yrs now, yrs

cutter holds it up and kisses it

granda   gave this to her when i first took her up for the carnival all those years back.

she were about yr age now.

man, she loved to dance! truly made her happy.

wanted to take her back to the islands, to trini, yu understand?
cutter   leave this cold and grey behind
granda   wanted to give her the sun.

in the end all i could give was carnival
cutter   but she loved to dance
granda   she were the carnival queen. everyone gave way to her as she danced these same streets. it was like she owned 'em – the streets, the sounds
cutter   ma ma: the carnival queen!

granda starts coughing, holding chest

cutter   quit foolin

granda sits on the curb and starts wheezing, gasping, spitting.

cutter   oh jeez. help. someone. quick.

cutter races off, and then runs back on with a bottle of red-stripe

granda *(drinking, then rubbing bottle on forehead)* aaah. that's better

cutter christ-man. yu orright. i mean. yu had me goin there. i thought ...

granda not gettin any younger is all. that and the mines, the minin, it took a lot outta me, yu know

he holds out his arm, cutter helps him up, then they dance

granda *(offering drink)* granddaughter, granddaughter, let's finish this up. eh?

cutter drinks, then splutters

granda first time up to carnival since yu was just a tot but it's not gonna be our last time eh?

cutter whaddya mean our last?

granda yu and me gal ... and the carnival.
just like ol' times.
now when i were yr age takin to the streets for carnival back home in trini – it was a riot! grand.

cutter weren't yu scared?

granda man! i was in the thick of it. their look-out

cutter what yu said earlier

granda yu got boxers feet. yu stand strong

granda dances / flirts

cutter, embarrassed, pulls him away.

cutter maan!

granda what?

cutter don't make a scene!

granda that's what carnivals for! when slavery ended we really took it back!

cutter slavery? yr not that old

granda yu cheeky / wee ... that one? got her eye on me

cutter   sooo embarrassin

granda *(starting to remove top)* i'll show yu embarrassin

cutter   she's not yr age

granda   what age's that?

granda staggers

cutter *(goes to help him)* yr no gonna pull like that!

granda *(pushin her away)* quit yr fussin woman, / quit yr

cutter / first time yu've called me woman!

granda   lass. girl. what difference it / make?

cutter / grandma. ma. me. three generations woman

granda   well

cutter   what?

granda   forget it

cutter   i'm no gonna forget.

yr goin down doctors' for check-up.

granda   they can't. help

cutter   don't mean gettin older.

but with yu fallin. twice now.

and yu'd hardly had a drop!

granda   doctors can't help

silence

cutter   what yu sayin?

silence

granda   yr right. yr gonna have to be a woman

cutter   what yu on about?

granda   yu know how it is with us miners.

cutter   no i don't know *(imitating)* how it is with us miners

granda   less yr cheek

cutter   how is it with yu miners?

granda	the mines, minin, dust: ... i'm all choked up ... *(touching lungs)* in here. / never
cutter	/ yu?
granda	a right time to tell .... it's never the / right time
cutter	/ yu??
granda	had check-up when yu was gettin *(reaches out to touch)* yr hair done / suits yu
cutter	/ 'sake!
granda	there's a cloud of coal dust claggin / me up
cutter	/ christ!
granda	shadows on me lungs, inhalin all that dust, that dirt
cutter	not yu too
granda	relax girl. i've years left

cutter hits granda in the chest with flat of her hand repeatedly

cutter	that's what they said over ma. *(hit)*. what they said and then ... *(hit)* more shadows on her breasts. *(hit)* and taken back to the hospital *(hit)* only there was nothin left to cut, to cut out. *(hit)* cancers all over, it's all over and
granda	weren't easy lass, but i did best i could. i love yu
cutter	dressin me in black. only time yu dressed me up
granda	i've dressed yu in carnival colors girl ... woman

cutter starts boxing, granda blocks – a boxing exercise, sparring across the stage

cutter	yu didnt ... tell me about blood
granda	jab jab left
cutter	who could i come to about boy-trouble?
granda	jab left jab right
cutter	girl-trouble eh?
granda	swing and

granda holds her tight

granda won't let yu down girl, i wont ... did all i could for yr
ma, ma daughter.
i didnt let her down ... and i'm not gonna ... not for
years

cutter runs off

granda goes after cutter

*cutter re-enters and sinks to knees, looks for something to cut
with*

*cutter pulls up sleeves exposing cuts / scars / plaster. (first view
should shock)*

granda *(entering)* what in the name of hell is this?

granda grabs her arms

cutter pulls away

cutter leave me be, leave me be

granda yr ma flesh, ma blood

cutter this is mine, flesh, mine – blood. but yu don't buy
the tampax so what dya know?

granda what in hells goin on? who done this to yu? gimme
their names

cutter no

granda what d'ya mean no?

silence

granda yu didn't ... yu couldn't? not y'rself?

cutter sometimes i get so low

granda yr gonna stop / this now

cutter *(collapsing into his arms)* / i miss ma

granda *(stroking her hair)* ma daughter, yr ma, i miss her too but i'm no leavin ... just gotta take it easy, yu too.

cutter   take it easy: that's the best doctors can give yu?

granda   can't believe no flesh and blood of mine ... *(touching bandages)* since when?

cutter   i love yu.

granda   know yu do girl, i know yu do

granda kisses the locket gently.

cutter kisses locket.

granda   yr ma's. ma daughters. ma daughter. and now it's yrs, ma treasure, now it's yrs.

cutter   cos ma's gone / and

granda   / i miss her too yu know. *(thumps chest)* miss her here like hell

cutter   i'm lonely, and no-one to hold me tight, to talk about all those things

granda   shoosh girl

cutter   soon i'll have no-one

granda *(lifting cutter's arms)* this has got to stop

he dances her gently off

four. boxin and losin

cutter	yr cryin granda
granda	man: just coal dust in me eye
cutter	nothin wrong with a man cryin
granda	rememberin the mine. the cut. the scar. the seam. is all
cutter	the cuttin gear. the steady hand. cut
granda	scar. seam. coal. the fire
cutter	steady-hand-cut
granda	scar. seam. cut-coal. fire
cutter	the clarity. lack of pain. mind-fog clears
granda	fire, fired-up.
cutter	see clearly now. feel
granda	seam of coal. the burn of coal
cutter	feel the burn
granda	survival
cutter	how ya think i got ma bloody name?
granda	half a century ago this port were alive. now everythin's dyin. gotta fight it man, yu gotta fight
cutter	still the grief here. pain here
granda	jab jab left jab right jab right
cutter	learnin to fight. there's discipline. art. it's not kickin off against some gobby lad two years older and twice yr size
granda	jab jab left jab right
cutter	granda taught some good moves. hell: yu taught the best
granda	*(holding up fists)* boxer's knuckles. and what makes 'em think yr any less a fighter girl? what makes 'em think yr no gonna fight? blow on yr knuckles, blow: cool the bruises, the bruisin down

cutter	sometimes wanna have ma hair braided fine ... but sometimes yeah *(punching fists together)* need to fight
granda	boxers knuckles since before the war, the mines, long before.

was the islands where yu had to fight!

now centre yrself. feel yr weight thru to yr feet.

think of how yr gonna drive. shoulders; torso; legs.

but start from stillness and ... hold it, hold it ... now

cutter/granda *(cutter boxing)* left right left right. left left. jab jab. swing. right right left and

granda   shoulders down and in ... and more feelin

cutter/granda   left right left left right

granda *(holding out fists)* see here: boxer's knuckles.

how they warp and flutter. bone misshapen.

bone cracked, bone-snap, scrap scrap.

scrapes of bone where none should be inside ma scrapped fist and ... what makes 'em think yr any less a fighter girl?

cutter	i fear
granda	fear
cutter	i wish
granda	wish
cutter	i dream
granda	dream
cutter	i fear fallin for ever

wish i'd stop fallin

i dream fallin

wish i'd stop

i dream the fall

i fear what comes after

granda   don't fear

cutter	i dream there's nothin after. fear nothin comes after
granda	don't fear what comes after. don't fear / that
cutter	i fear that. i wish there was somethin after
granda	we all have wishes.

and tho wishes are secret i couldn't-of wished for a better lass.

forged like the crush of coal, a diamond: fierce cuttin to sheer thru any surface.

strong, proud, true. *(rubbing chin)*

and hell-of-an uppercut! now get in there

cutter	miss jones. granda. ringside. her not lookin.

his grin. me butterflyin. them both shoutin

granda/cutter *(shouting)* get in there. and win!

cutter enters ring

granda   laydeez, gennelmen in the back corner: lemme hear a big hand ... i said lemme hear yu ...

cutter punching air

granda   that's better ... the rebel star, swansea snarler, queen of the m4, avenger of the valleys, cutter! we know yu got the poetry within – we seen yr footwork!

so what's the rap on yu girl? what's the rap on yu?

cutter   choose to fight or yu can choose flight

or bury yr head cos life's too great a fright

but we all gotta choice in the rules we live by

we all got choice in the rules we live by

they call me cutter and i've just turned 18

but was taught by greatest fighter i've ever seen

he taught me to fight hard but fair take on yr rules

cos we all got some choice in how we get by

granda   a big round for cu-tter cu-tter cu-tter

cutter   i'm gonna throw some punches before i lie down
                i'm gonna throw some punches before i die down

bell rings

cutter starts to box

granda *(commentating)* round three and level on points, each
                lookin for the knock-out and now ... circlin, circlin.
                cutter may not have the reach but she's sure got
                speed and. oh no.
                cutter stumbles recovers and ... they're back up
                lookin for an openin lookin to open up
                feint drive drive in reach skin, open up and yes
                did yu see that oh killer maan killer. yes.
                now weavin defensive doin the dance the dance
                it's in the stance
                get yr body behind in good and fast and out again
                i taught her that cu-tter
                cu-tter and they're really squarin off to it now.
                oooooh vicious.
                the glints gone from cutter's eyes.
                a cut above her eye, streamin blood it's is it it's i
                think yes ref's callin a halt
                aaaaah she could-of
                could-of been ...
                young too young yr ma dyin when yu ... she ...
                was too young ... taught yu best i could girl but that
                weren't enough
cutter   yu let me wear yr boxin gloves
granda   yr wee hands in ma old gloves
cutter   yr boxin gloves, huge. yr huge hands, warm
granda   yu got her face lass, her looks
cutter   really?!

granda	but yu got muscles. she didn't have yr strength
cutter	i really do look like her?
granda	she didn't
cutter	i really look?
granda	aye. but she weren't tough like yu. yu gotta be strong to survive this.
cutter	ma washin blood off me first time i fell and cut hands open
granda	yr ma could dance! she got the rhythm of trini in her
cutter	and i don't?
granda	yu got yr own rhythm. a strong true powerful rhythm
cutter	but ma?
granda	she could dance but she weren't tough like yu. she couldnt stand up to ... a time to fight lass, a time to fight.
cutter	but it's so bloody hard just turnin 18 and so so alone.
granda	a time to fight lass, and a time ... time to ... to let go

five. serial killers

granda   lung cancer from breathin in all that crap down the mines. they took me into hospital to die.

said *(imitating)* 'it was for the best'.

hospital stank of biscuits, tea and piss: enough to kill anybody

got out ma bed walked thru to where they was lyin there stoned on out-of-date loraz, lorazepam watchin

(tv voice)   serial killers on itv

(own voice) maaan! turned back to ma bed. lay down.

laughed. gallows humor. i guess.

that tv! on all hours, too loud. fixed to top gear, mass murder or casualty.

drillin dross into ma head till i wanna scream.

i'm dyin and there's no peace, none at all.

packed ma stuff into those green hospital carrier bags.

signed maself out against their advice.

they tried keepin me in to die. *(imitating)* 'it is for the best.'

went out front waitin on ma granddaughter, on her takin me home

cutter enters, takes granda's bag and carries it for him

she came and took me home ...

a good lass. really she is. the best

home to die ... and in this – no more fear, even.

no time to fear.

on ma way out, can feel it within.

years of regrets, those bloody mines

great dark clouds of dust invadin ma body.

but the time for fear is past.

only question left is what will become of ma granddaughter? what will become of her?

six. samaritans

granda   all i wanted was one last good coal fire
            she banked the flames up good like i'd taught,
            stokin the flames, i knew then i could let go

cutter   by the end he weighed less than an angel and like
            one he kept flyin off
            me pullin him back, tellin him he had no shift
            how much did the lungs they cut out weigh?
            and he never even smoked
            tuckin blanket round his shoulders and sittin beside
            him till the harsh suck at air quietens to sleep and
            next thing either of us knew would be mornin post

granda/cutter   bills. electricity. water. poll tax. tv.

(advertiser's voices) yu have won. yu may have won.
            apply now. reduced. interest-transfer. interest-free.
            special rates.
            how about a loan a car language course a spanish
            holiday nice new dress a boob-job?

granda   how about stuffin it? i'd use those letters to light
            our front room fire, all that junk to get the coal
            alight

cutter   to feel somethin. anythin. nothin.
            they say we shouldn't harm others, harm ourselves.
            don't they see i only want to ... sometimes just to
            feel ... to feel somethin, to feel anythin...
            or to feel nothin
            and ma died and now granda's dyin and i've no-one
            and i'm scared so scared
            there's no life for me now but the cut: to feel;
            somethin; anythin; nothin
            takin glass from the gutter to ma arms.
            bone-hard, knife-steady.

an absence leavin its neat line.

or cut sometimes because the alternatives worse

how d'ya think i got ma name.

and how it stuck?

granda   cuttin coal from the seam.

this black crushed to a brilliant, perfect blade.

cutter   granda would always carry a bag for bits of coal. then at the end on his knees strugglin to light the fire and me sayin here and kindlin it *(with a sheet of newspaper)* just so.

a sheet from yesterday's mornin star to draw air up chimney.

(rocking sheet of newspaper) the suck of air, the rasp of his breath, and then ... no breathin, no breath.

i turn, turn to him

cutter crumples paper into ball

granda leaves

cutter   only he was gone ... soaked his wool cardie thru as i sobbed and sobbed, and not wantin to let go cryin cryin, fire dyin, but he was gone ... *(crumplin paper into phone shape)* only then did i make the call

strugglin to keep goin. sleepless nights.

doctor sees me lookin like i'd gone 13 rounds with mohammed ali – granda and my greatest boxer of all time, says somethin to relax yu, writes me up for these little blue pills.

chemist peerin sure these are for yu?

and goin to phone surgery till he recognises us – 'oh! yr kane's grandchild ... i was sorry to hear yr ... he whispers ... loss.' and passes over me tablets.

and i'm numb to it all and cleanin out granda's
medicines – his painkillers lyin there but

granda *(off)* that's no answer. no answer at all

there's no angels singin, no harps and clouds
no tunnels of bright white light

cutter   in the end i dials samaritans ... 084 57

granda *(off)* jab

cutter   90

granda *(off)* jab

cutter   90

granda *(off)* left

cutter   90

granda *(off)* jab right jab right

cutter   rng

granda *(off)* hook cut

cutter   c'mon answer will ya

granda *(off)* upper cut

cutter   rng rng rng

granda *(off)* jab right jab right

cutter   just bloody answer i cry out as this sweet voice picks
up

granda *(off)* hook cut and

cutter   and i'm sobbin, what i'm feelin like, why.

so low-down; can't sleep; can't eat; eyein up them
tablets and samaritans just listenin till finally: can i
call hospital?

get yu somewhere safe for a while?

i whispers ... safe .... yessss.

and so i'm admitted – community psychiatric ward
– just till i gets back on me feet

seven. fight-back

cutter *(rocking)* it's all ma fault: i'm tellin the psychiatrists that. ma fault – granda's dyin – especially that. hospital said he was gonna … but miracles happen. every week, people live. now i'm the last, the last one in me family, last of ma family and i wanna cut thru ma flesh, let the grief flow so bad, only this hospital – they won't even allow that.

and manic street preachers ritchie carvin for real into his arm and needin 27 stitches and i close ma eyes, imagine gettin as far as england, the severn bridge, and jumpin – but i just can't. and some folks say he's still alive – runnin a chippie in carmarthen, a bookies in bangor, impersonatin elvis in aber. truth is he's long gone; but then it's different if yr a pop-star.

me? 18 and no family and no home and alone and so so hard, and yu don't know where to turn not like when yu was wee and granda there to hold yr hand, pick yu up when yu fall, ice cream and fruit salad and sparklers on yr birthday. so bloody hard to fight on thru

granda *(off)* show me respeck and i'll respeck yu back.

but treat me like animal and i become one

cutter there's this bloody nazi logo, bnp, on the hospital walls and i want the fascist thing off. needs a marker-pen to line it out only all the markers are locked in the office, so i asks, gets turned down. nurse sayin: yu and yr kind: just keep it quiet *(running and screaming)* fuuuuuuuuuuuuk

cutter punches the wall hard, breaks a finger

cutter nurses her broken hand

granda enters, taping up fingers, massaging them for her

granda   yu bust it girl, yu bust it. why harm yrself. why?
          we weren't put on the earth for this

cutter   cutters ma name

granda   it ennt yr name is it?

cutter   tis now

granda   c'mon louise eh ... such a nice, lasses name ...
          what's the angle? what else cuts? a good cut, a
          clean cut, another way of seein ...

cutter   ... diamonds, s'pose: ... they cut. cut thru everythin

granda   right yu are. and?

cutter   all those mines, shafts cut out the hill. cuttin out the
          coal

granda   lightin up the world

cutter   and granda said i'd a wicked upper-cut. caught him
          with it sometimes.

granda   there's a reason yr here: we don't want yu hurt. we
          want yu strong again yeah?

cutter   granda, he showed me this piece of coal he had
          mined, sayin it's black is precious like yu ma wee
          star he said. 'precious like yr ma'. 'precious like yu
          too granda' i say...
          i said, as he held it gentle to ma skin.

granda   this coal is black, precious, hundred-million-year-old
          tree, wee branches within.
          and don't forget coal crushed becomes the
          unstoppable blade of diamond

cutter / granda jab jab left jab right jab right cut hook cut snap
          yr wrists snap and back

cutter   and ma sweet stubborn fighter granda's gone.
          and me so weary, like the bottom of an endless pit
          shaft, no light. just wantin to sink.

granda: why did yu go leave me?

ma. why did yu die so long ago??

but then ... that nurse ... tapin ma hand up, bringin me back to life, remindin me of ma family, ma heritage, encouragin me to fight true, to fight on thru ... can't give up now, i cant.

that would be to condemn granda and ma, to condemn 'em both, and i can't do that.

cutter / granda jab jab left

jab right

snap yr wrists snap back

snap and back

upper cut and

and jab right jab right

cutter nurse said i should get a first aid box. keep ma wounds clean

granda there's cuttin up rough girl ... and there's cuttin up sweet.

a time and a place for punches and for rollin with 'em ... now get out there. don't get distracted. don't take no. now's time to fight, fight back. yeah?

cutter yeah.

granda for real?

cutter for real.

granda swear?

cutter don't wanna slave no more

granda don't slave no more

cutter we all need some respeck in our life, nurse helpin me back, helpin me stop cuttin, lessenin ma depression, helpin me get ma respeck back.

now i gotta fight, fight on thru in ma and granda's memory, and i gotta, gotta win!

eight. keep yr neck in lass

cutter *(showing locket – now with picture of granda and ma in)*
granda took this locket off ma's neck when she lay
there dead, cold.

he put it round ma neck to warm it up, said he was
lookin for the right time to pass it on ... now i've his
picture in here too.

granda   find the spark louise. pits closed, but the coals still
there, deep underground, waitin to be cut free ...
and set alight

cutter   cold, so cold, like someone stepped on ma grave.
could do with one his fires now.

granda   find the spark louise, feel the burn

cutter   he used to say the coal seam remains under-ground,
yu just gotta find it again. christ, granda! i expected
somethin, wilder, grander: never thought yu'd go so
quiet ... boxin's a dance, aye? well i'm gonna dance
those same sands. dance for him. for ma. for me.
i'm gonna, gonna dance me own dance

granda   yu got broad shoulders louise but keep yr neck in
girl, keep yr neck in. yu cartwheelin on sands; yr
bird-cries answerin the gulls ... or takin yu nottin hill
like those carnivals of ma youth back in trinidad,
trini. aah! calypsos and chutney music and fusin
that to soca; magnificent sound systems, and
dancin, dancin, till i collapsed and yu searchin
crowd for help and them passed a bottle of cold
cold red-stripe – aaah, ma star, ma wee star, and
of-course each day readin the *mornin star*: first
words yu ever read

cutter / granda *mo-r-nin staah!*

cutter   first mornin in that hospital and i'm rememberin on
all this. and then this nazi skin with hate and more
as his knuckles tattoo mornin paper mornin paper.

granda yu would-of hit out, i remembered yr fight 'em girl, but i lashed out with me tongue instead. orders the communist paper off that fascist-skin, ma words sinkin in, scorchin his skin. *mornin star. mornin star.* comrade

cutter makes the clenched fist salute

aah granda yu didn't believe in heaven, god or owtt but i reckon yr smilin now. could feel the fear and the fury burnin up in me, the adrenalin surge like before a big fight, adrenalin surgin – so i used words - drivin their uppercut right in

hey mister nazi yr really not that clever

think yr war of slogans gonna trigger somethin big

well it's yu doin the diggin

granda   diggin deep then deeper

cutter   followin yr nose to the sewage down below

granda   followin yr nose to the sewage below

cutter   well i've news for yu, little feller

i've somethin big n better

granda   she's got fire in her fingertips

cutter   i've fire in ma mind

i've fire in ma fists

and ma tongues not far behind

cutter / granda keep diggin and remember if yu come up for air

cutter   i'll be there

granda   beware

cutter   cos i've fire in ma fingertips

fire in ma mind

cutter / granda i've fire in ma boxin

cutter   and ma tongues not far behind

ma tongues not far behind

oh granda. i was rockin out, tears from ma eyes,
and this cool nurse, practically dancin along, smilin.
we touched knuckles. respeck!

granda   a little truth. sometimes it's enough to get yr respeck
back.

cutter begins bandaging her fists ready for the boxing

then clenching /unclenching fist

now punching fist into hand

*her arms are now free of any cutting bandages and her hands
are bound for a fight*

cutter   to conquer the cut. to fight ma grief, beat ma
depression. in granda's memory. in ma's memory.
in my own. on my own. bring it on bring it on

granda   laydeez, gennelmen in the black corner: the rebel
star, swansea snarler, avenger of the valleys, she
always shall be: our very own lou-iiise ... big yrself
up girl, big yrself up

cutter   i was taught by the greatest fighter i've ever seen
he taught fight hard but fair and yu'll get respeck
back
we all got choice in the rules we live by
and i'm gonna throw some punches
i'm not gonna lie down
gonna give ma best shot not gonna die down

again cutter boxing

granda *(commentating)* they're really squarin off to it now,
the glint in louise's eyes.
jab jab left jab right jab
right jab right jab right.

and cut oh vicious yes.

speed of that cut – what a blow.

yu heard the crunch!

louise is standin tall, standin proud, her opponents down, she's down.

they're countin her out, countin her out. lou-ise louise has won.

she's won. she has won!

cutter i'm alive. i'm alive! and i'm dedicatin this win to ma and granda, to 'em both, to their memory

granda yu know wishes are secret, aye? well (*pointing at cutter*) i got ma wish and ... louise, somehow she's gonna get hers

cutter witness the healin

granda the cut – gone; scar – gone; seam – gone

cutter ma hand won't obey the blade

granda coal gone, mines gone, long gone

cutter won't obey the blade, ma hand wont

granda community gone

cutter blade gone

granda pit wheels no longer turn

cutter release me: i see clearly, feel, the blade gone

granda the scar grassed over

cutter witness to the healin

granda kneels before her, unwrapping hands

cutter show me respeck and i show respeck back eh?

granda i want to take yu and (*lifting her up*) ... show yu the sun

lights down

the end.

GRANDMOTHER'S CLOSET by Luke Hereford
ISBN 978-1-912430-89-5   £8.99

THE CONVERT by Ben Kavanagh
ISBN 978-1-912430-76-5   £9.99

NEXT LESSON by Chris Woodley
ISBN 978-1-912430-19-2   £9.99

CARE TAKERS by Billy Cowan
9781910798-81-2   £9.99

BREATHLESS by Laura Horton
ISBN 978-1-912430-83-3   £8.99

NOOR by Azma Dar
ISBN 978-1-912430-72-7   £9.99

THE MAKING OF A MONSTER by Connor Allen
ISBN 978-1-912430-85-7   £9.99

FREE-FALL by Ashwin Singh
ISBN 978-1-911501-07-7   £9.99

THREE WOMEN by Matilda Velevitch
ISBN 978-1-912430-35-2   £9.99

PROJECT XXX by Kim Wiltshire & Paul Hine
ISBN 978-1-906582-55-5   £8.99

COMBUSTION by Asif Khan
ISBN 978-1-911501-91-6   £9.99

DIARY OF A HOUNSLOW GIRL by Ambreen Razia
ISBN 978-0-9536757-9-1   £8.99

SPLIT/MIXED by Ery Nzaramba
ISBN 978-1-911501-97-8   £10.99

THE TROUBLE WITH ASIAN MEN by Sudha Bhuchar, Kristine
Landon-Smith and Louise Wallinger
ISBN 978-1-906582-41-8   £8.99

More great plays at:
www.aurorametro.com